Renée H. Guillory, Editor

*Wild at Hearth:*
*Arizona Recipes for the*
*Kitchen and the Trail*

IBSN: 0-615-12490-9

# ACKNOWLEDGMENTS

For more than 40 years, the Grand Canyon Chapter of the Sierra Club has answered the call to explore, enjoy and protect Arizona. Their conservation programs guard the Grand Canyon, one of the world's most unique ecosystems, as well as many other grand places in Arizona – whether they are in our neighborhoods or alongside a rare, quiet desert rivulet, or atop a sky island peak.

It is to the members of the Grand Canyon Chapter of the Sierra Club – as well as to its loyal volunteers and staff – that this book is dedicated. Many of them donated the family recipes included here.

All proceeds from the sale of this cookbook will go to benefit programs that make Arizona's cities more livable and that protect the many public lands and wild places that nourish us.

# TABLE OF CONTENTS

Wild At Hearth

# FOREWORD

The turn of the 21st century is witnessing an explosion of interest and concern about how and what we eat, how we manage farms and rangelands, how we treat farm animals, and how the pace of our lives ultimately determines our relationship with food and cooking.  It's a renaissance of sorts, perhaps as important as the invention of restaurants in 18th century France.

A movement based on the melding of environmental and social aspects of food, the so-called Slow Food movement, is gaining strength around the world, and not a minute too soon.

Today, the bulk of our food is produced anonymously, industrially, with more concern for shelf life and volume than for the long-term health and productivity of the land or for "the pleasures of the table," to use an old phrase.

As Gary Nabhan notes in his introduction, just one of the benefits of preparing fresh foods and getting to know the local farmers who provide our meals' raw material is to create more accountability in food production.  Raising livestock and operating confined animal feed lots (CAFOs) are prickly issues in the arid Southwest.  Knowing how animals are raised and what the landscape, the fragile river ecosystems, and the human communities bear in that process allows consumers to choose producers who are better stewards.

Not all the recipes I've collected here specifically focus on historically important Southwestern foods – my own crawfish etouffée is a case in point – but they do convey a love for preparing meals with fresh ingredients that reflect the many food traditions of the contributors while accommodating those pesky busy schedules and outdoor travel plans. The section on web-based resources guides us to local farmers' markets throughout Arizona, which is an excellent way to experiment with how the Southwest tastes when making these family recipes.

***Wild at Hearth*** takes us a small step in the direction of more thoughtful, Slow eating and cooking in the home or on outings: cooking that has both conservation and great taste in mind. *Bon appetit*!

– R.H.G.
Phoenix, Arizona

# INTRODUCTION

Environmental advocates sometimes wonder how their food choices affect land stewardship and biodiversity conservation. The ways are many; what you choose to eat is not merely a hedonistic act, it is a political and ecological act, favoring good land and water stewardship, or alternatively, leading us down desolation row.

Let's offer a few examples from Arizona. While some farms draw upon rainfed and local surface water diversions, others consume huge quantities of water from long-distance river diversions and groundwater overpumping. By visiting farms where your food comes from, you can sense whether their water use is sustainable.

Cattle and sheep are not intrinsically damaging to the environment or healing of it; it is how they are managed. By eating feedlot beef, you are vulnerable to all the atrocities cited in the bestseller, *Fast Food Nation*. By purchasing predator-friendly, certified organic or pasture-raised beef, pork or chicken, you are voting with your wallet for ranchlands that are managed with minimal impact on wildlife, and for healthier foods as well.

Sourcing more of your wild and cultivated foods from local sources means that you can bike by and see how your food is being grown. You can also reduce the fossil fuel waste, carbon emissions and contamination susceptibility associated with long-distance transport of foods. The average food travels 1500 hundred miles before it hits the lips of the typical American. The amount of food Americans eat that is raised in other countries has doubled in the last 8 years, where environmental regulations are less strict than in our own region.

Eating local means that our food has a traceable human face and a story associated with it. Enjoy more locally-grown food as well as the stories surrounding them, for they will enrich you!

Gary Nabhan, author of *Coming Home to Eat*
Alta Arizona Slow Food leader
Director, Center for Sustainable Environments
at Northern Arizona University

*"Every recipe is a story with a happy ending."*

Mark Harris

# Appetizers

# Southwest Camping Appetizer I
## by Elna Otter
## Tucson

1 can cheddar cheese soup
1 can* chopped green chiles (mild or hot, to taste)
Blue corn or other interesting taco chips.

Heat the soup in a small saucepan over medium heat. Once soup is warmed through, add chiles and then adjust seasoning if desired. Pour into dipping bowl and serve with chips while still warm.

* Substitution: Roast (discard charred skins and seeds) and chop 2 large green chiles in place of canned chiles – these are easily available throughout Arizona in season.

# Southwest Appetizer II
## by Elna Otter
## Tucson

Yield: approximately 50 pieces

1 can cheddar cheese soup
1 can* chopped green chiles (mild or hot, to taste)
Tortillas

Mix cheese soup and chiles by hand or with electric mixer. Adjust seasoning if desired. Spread thinly on tortillas, making sure they are completely covered. Roll up tortillas and chill. Just before serving cut rolls into 1/2" pieces. (The preparer gets to eat the end pieces.)

* Substitution: Roast (discard charred skins and seeds) and chop 2 large green chiles in place of canned chiles – these are easily available throughout Arizona in season.

# Los Olivos (The Olives)
## by Jim McCarthy
## Flagstaff


Yield:  one jar of olives

Olives
Several cloves of split garlic
Dried oregano
Salt water



     Collect mature olives from a cooperative tree.  In Phoenix, they are about right in September.  Harvest olives that are as ripe as possible, without being soft.

     Hit the olives with a blunt object enough to split them, or cut two opposite sides of each olive with a knife.

     Soak the olives in salt water for ten days – long enough to remove the bitterness.  To prepare the salt water, first determine how much water is necessary to cover the olives completely.  Dissolve just enough salt in your fresh water until an egg floats.  Remove the egg and add the olives to the salt water.  Prepare new salt water every day or two during the salt bath.  (A large porcelain stew pot with lid works really well.)

     On day eleven, drain the olives and prepare the final salt water.  Place olives, salt water, several cloves of split garlic (let your palate be your guide), and a few shakes of dried oregano into a canning jar; depending on your harvest, you may need several canning jars – simply multiply the garlic and oregano as needed.  Store at room temperature or in a cooler.  Enjoy often!

# Stuffed Celery
by Bertha Cook
Cornville

Yield:  about one dozen stuffed celery sticks

In a food processor, cream together:
4 oz  bleu cheese
4 tbsp sour cream
Dash of Worcestershire sauce

Wash, trim, and pat dry the amount of celery you'd like to prepare for your dinner party.  Cut celery into 2-3" lengths.   Stuff celery sticks using a pastry tube and bag.

This recipe multiplies easily.

*"There is no love sincerer than the love of food."*

Bernard Shaw

# Roasted Grapes, Olives, and Nuts
## by Leigh Blakemore
## Scottsdale Culinary Institute
## Scottsdale

Yield: 4 portions
Preheat: 350°F

2 cups seedless grapes, washed, stems removed
1 cup walnuts or pecans (halves)
1 cup mixed picholine and oil cured olives
2 tbsp Balsamic vinegar
2 tbsp olive oil
3 sprigs thyme, stems removed
1 lemon thin-sliced, with seeds removed
kosher salt

Combine all ingredients in a small baking dish. Bake uncovered for about 45 minutes, stirring occasionally: pay attention, for grapes should be wilted but not deflated. Once baked, lemon slices will have dissolved leaving the rind. Discard rind. Adjust seasoning and lightly stir again.

Chef's Note:

This dish is delicious served hot, warm or at room temperature. I serve this as an appetizer with some great cheese (Maytag Blue, brie, or goat cheese) and bread. It's also excellent as part of an antipasti course with traditional Italian tidbits like prosciutto, salami, pickled artichoke hearts, marinated mushrooms, small hot peppers, etc.

One of the most well recieved ways I've served it is as a side dish with a traditional Swiss cheese fondue. The sweet, sour, crunchy components of the dish are a perfect contrast to the strong favor and creamy texture of the swiss cheese and Kirsch combination of the fondue. Enjoy!

# Salads, Side Dishes, and Breads

# Mashed Potato Salad
## by Jean Berringer
## Phoenix

Yield:  6-8 portions

4-6 large potatoes, boiled, peeled, and mashed
1 hard-boiled egg, chopped
1/4 cup sweet pickle relish
1 tsp dry mustard, ground
1 small onion, chopped
1/2 cup mayonnaise
salt and freshly ground pepper to taste
1 sliced hard-boiled egg
paprika

Mix first five ingredients well.   Add mayonnaise and mix until a smooth, creamy consistency is reached.   Add seasonings to taste. Top with sliced hard-boiled egg.   Sprinkle paprika over all.


Chef's Note:

This is a classic dish and a midwestern family favorite.

# Three Corners Cucumber Salad
## by Lee Oler
## Tucson, AZ

Yield: 4 portions

2 good-sized cucumbers, peeled and sliced
1 cup sugar
1/2 cup vinegar
1/4 cup water
1/2 small red onion, sliced thinly

Mix the sugar, vinegar, and water together in a medium saucepan and bring to a boil. Let cool, then pour over sliced cucumbers. Chill. In a large serving dish, layer cucumbers and onions. Pour some of the liquid over the salad. Chill for several hours before serving.

Chef's Note:

This recipe survives thanks to Mrs. Elma Lewis. She originally brought this Wyoming family recipe to Arizona by way of Colorado.

*"Tell me what you eat, and I will tell you what you are."*

Jean Anthelme Brillat-Savarin

# Blue's Potatoes
by Kyrsten Sinema
Phoenix

Yield: 4 portions

olive oil
2 large or 3 small potatoes, chopped
1/2 large red onion, chopped
1 clove garlic, diced
1 cup sliced mushrooms
1 tbsp chopped fresh basil
salt and pepper or your favorite seasoning
shredded cheese (optional)
organic ketchup

Line the bottom of a skillet with a thin sheet of olive oil. Add chopped potatoes and cook covered for 10 minutes on medium heat, stirring occasionally to brown evenly. Stir in onions, cook uncovered for 5 minutes. Stir in sliced mushrooms, cook uncovered for 5 minutes. Stir in diced garlic, cook uncovered for several minutes. Add chopped basil, cook uncovered for several minutes. Stir throughout.

Season lightly with salt and pepper or your favorite seasoning, then remove from heat. If using cheese, sprinkle on top of potatoes without stirring upon removal from heat.

Spoon generously on plates, and eat with plenty of organic ketchup.

# Arizona Vortex Mashed Sweet Potatoes
### by Heidi Slagle
### Phoenix

Preheat: 375°F

one potato per serving; multiply ingredients as needed
1/8 cup butter
1/4 cup orange juice
1 tsp light brown sugar
1/8 tsp each of cinnamon, nutmeg and pumpking pie spice
large marshmallows

Boil sweet potatoes until soft in a large pot - drain and mash,
adding butter. Gently place mashed potatoes into a buttered
baking dish. Stir in orange juice and add light brown sugar. Add
cinnamon, nutmeg and pumpkin pie spice, which contains some
ginger to add energy (vortex!). Mix it all thoroughly and then dot
top with large marshmallows. Bake until marshmallows melt and
turn brown.

# Zucchini casserole
## by Rich & Claire Genser
## Tucson

Yield:  4 portions
Preheat:  350°F

4 zucchini
1/2 cup butter or margarine
1 pint sour cream (or lite sour cream)
1/2 cup grated cheddar
1 tsp mustard
1/2 cup bread crumbs

Slice zucchini and steam until soft.  Place steamed zucchini in casserole dish or in individual casserole dishes.  Add butter or margarine and stir until butter is melted.  Add mustard, grated cheese and sour cream and stir well.  Add all but 2-3 tbsps of bread crumbs and stir.  Mixture should not be too much of a liquid. If it is, add more bread crumbs and stir until mixture is thick.  Top with remaining bread crumbs and bake for 15 minutes.

*"You don't have to cook fancy or complicated masterpieces – just good food from fresh ingredients."*

Julia Child

# Artichokes with Garlic and Herb Butter
## by Boxed Greens*
## Tempe

Yield: 2 portions

2 artichokes
Salt to taste
3 oz butter
1 garlic clove, crushed
1 tbsp assorted fresh or dried herbs (your preference)
lemon wedges

Wash artichokes well in cold water. Using a sharp knife, cut the stalks level with the bases. Snip off the pointed ends of the top of the chokes with kitchen scissors. Put the prepared artichokes in a large saucepan of lightly salted water. Bring to a boil, cover, and cook about 45 minutes or until a lower leaf comes away when gently pulled. Drain artichokes upside down while preparing the sauce.

Melt the butter over low heat, add the garlic and cook for 30 seconds. Remove from heat and stir in the herbs and then spoon into one or two small serving bowls. Place the artichokes on plates and serve with the dipping sauce. Garnish with lemon wedges.

*Used with permission

# Stir-Fried Asian Greens
## by Boxed Greens*
### Tempe

Yield: 4 portions

1 tbsp peanut oil
1 tsp roasted peanut oil
1 tbsp minced garlic
1 tsp ground ginger
1/2 tsp crushed red pepper flakes
2 tbsp chopped scallions
6-10 cups fresh greens
1/2 cup stock  (vegetable or chicken)
salt
2 tbsp dark sesame oil
1 tsp rice wine or medium dry sherry
1 tsp cornstarch diluted with 3 tbsp water or stock

Heat a wok or large skillet and add both peanut oils.  When hot, add the garlic, ginger, red pepper flakes and scallions.  Stir-fry for 30 seconds, then add the greens and stir-fry for 1 minute more. Add the stock, cover and steam until tender, about 2 to 3 minutes. Season with salt, sesame oil and rice wine.

Letting the juices fall back into the wok, lift the greens with tongs and set them on a platter.  Add the cornstarch to the juices left in the wok and boil until thickened.  Pour the sauce over the greens.

*Used with permission

# Greens with Potatoes
## by Boxed Greens*
## Tempe

Yield: 4 portions

1 lb boiling potatoes
1-2 handsful or bunches of mixed greens, coarsely chopped
2 tbsp extra virgin olive oil, plus extra for finishing
1 large garlic clove, thinly sliced
1/2 tsp red pepper flakes
1-2 tomatoes, peeled and diced

Cover the potatoes with cold water, add salt to taste and bring to a boil. Cook until tender, about 25 minutes. Drain, then peel and coarsely chop. Simmer the greens in a large skillet until tender, then drain. You may need to do this in two batches. Return the skillet to the stove, add the oil, and heat with the garlic and pepper flakes. When you can smell the garlic, add the greens, potatoes, and tomatoes. Cook over medium heat, breaking up the potatoes with a fork and mashing them into the greens to make a kind of rough hash. Taste for salt and serve with olive oil drizzled over the top.

*Used with permission

# Pain au chou  (Cabbage Gratin)
## by Boxed Greens*
## Tempe

Yield:  4 portions
Preheat: 375°F

Butter
Freshly grated parmesan cheese
1 1/2 lbs green or savoy cabbage, diced into 2-inch pieces
1/3 cup flour
1 cup milk
1/4 cup cream
2 tbsp tomato paste
3 eggs
3 tbsp finely chopped parsely or dill
salt and freshly milled pepper

Butter a gratin dish and coat the sides with cheese.  Boil the
cabbage, uncovered, in salted water for about 5 minutes.  Drain.
Rinse, then press out excess water.

Whisk the remaining ingredients until smooth.  Add cabbage and
pour mixture into dish.  Bake until firm and lightly browned, about
50 minutes.

*Used with permission

About the gear:

An au gratin dish is typically a heavy  baking dish that is
porcelain-finished cast iron, which aids with even heating
and does not interfere with the flavors of the dish being
baked.  Usually, it is oval in shape and measures 14” x 2
1/2” (or thereabouts).

Of course, you can use a pyrex 13” x 13” x 2” baking pan
instead.  You will need to experiment with your oven to
determine the best baking time.

# Summer Squash Sauté
## by Boxed Greens*
## Tempe

Yield: 4 portions

1 lb sunburst squash or zucchini, cut in quarters
1 small onion, finely diced
2 cloves garlic, crushed
2 tbsp olive oil
1 pinch oregano
1-2 tomatoes, chopped with juice
1/3 cup feta or sharp cheddar cheese

Heat olive oil over medium-high heat in large skillet. Sauté garlic and onion until fragrant. Add squash and tomatoes and sauté until barely tender. Add oregano, reduce heat, and cover for about 5 minutes until tender. Turn off heat and stir in cheese and serve immediately.

Variations: Add green chiles or jalepeños for a spicier dish. This is also great served in tortillas with salsa on the side.

*Used with permission

*"To eat is a necessity, but to eat intelligently is an art."*

La Rochefoucauld

# Zucchini Bread
## Kathy Roediger
## Phoenix

Yield:  two loaves
Preheat:  350°F

1 cup brown sugar
1 cup sugar
1 cup vegetable oil
3 eggs
1 tsp vanilla
2 tsp maple flavoring
1 1/3 cup white flour
1 cup whole wheat flour
1 tsp baking soda
1 tsp salt
1/4 tsp baking powder
3 tsp cinnamon
2 cups grated raw zucchini
1 cup chopped nuts

Combine sugars, vegetable oil and eggs in a mixing bowl and beat until well-mixed.  Add vanilla and maple flavorings and mix well.  Add zucchini and mix well.  In a separate bowl, combine flours, soda, baking powder, salt and cinnamon.  Add dry ingredients to batter mixture gradually, beating after each addition.  Lastly, fold in nuts by hand.

Pour batter into two lightly oiled loaf pans and bake for about 1 hour; when loaves are done, an inserted toothpick should come out clean.

# Entrees

# Vegan Sonoran Spirals
## by Sandy Bahr
### Phoenix

2/3 cup peanut butter (or tahini)
3/4 cup water
3-4 tbsp soy sauce
2 tbsp rice vinegar (or lemon juice)
1 scallion, coarsely chopped (optional)
1 tbsp sweetener (optional as well)
1/2 tsp ground ginger
1/3 tsp chili powder (replace with 1/3 tsp chili oil for a sesame
        flavor or, alternately, use cumin)
12 oz uncooked spiral pasta
1 1/2 cups frozen peas

Combine first eight ingredients, mix well (food processor or blender works best.)  Cook pasta and peas according to instructions.  Combine.  Sauce is good over steamed vegetables and rice as well.

Chef's Note:

This recipe was given to me by Jennifer Anderson and it helped fortify me in the battle over Arizona's urban growth management initiative.  The work for growth management and saving the Sonoran Desert continues and therefore the need for more Sonoran Spirals.

# Fire Point Flambé
## by Sharon Galbreath
## Flagstaff

Yield:  4 portions

2 tbsp of olive oil or butter
2 medium shallots, thinly sliced
2 cloves of garlic, minced
2 to 3 fresh Roma tomatoes, chopped
a sprinkle of fresh or dried basil
salt and pepper
1 lb of raw shrimp, peeled and deveined
enough fettucini noodles or cooked rice to serve four
grated parmesan for garnish

Sauté the shallots and garlic in olive oil or butter over medium heat until soft. Add chopped tomatoes and basil continue cooking for two minutes. Add shrimp and sauté until shrimp are cooked. Season with salt and pepper to taste. Spoon over cooked pasta or rice with parmesan garnish and serve with salad and french bread.

Chef's Note:

The colors and flavor of this dish are a perfect accompaniment to the fiery colors of a Grand Canyon sunset reflecting off the golden bark of a stand of old growth ponderosa pine trees.  This simple main dish can be easily altered to feed vegans or vegetarians.

# Baja Casserole
## by Valarie J. Vousden
## Phoenix

Yield:  5-6 portions
Preheat:  400°F

2 1/4 cups chicken stock
2 cups long grain rice, rinsed
3 poblano chiles, cut in half, seeded
4 tomatillas, diced small
4 slices of bacon, chopped small
2 cloves of garlic, minced
5 scallions (green onions), chopped
Corn cut off one cob or  1 cup frozen corn
1/4 cup cilantro, chopped
6 oz of raw peeled & deveined shrimp
12 oz (total) shredded cheddar, monterey, asadero & queso
          blanco cheese OR Kraft's Mexican 4 Cheese mix
salt and pepper to taste

Boil chicken stock then add rice.  Cook for 15 minutes, medium
low, covered.  Place chiles on a baking sheet skin side up under
the broiler till nearly blackened, but not burned.  Put them in a
bowl with a lid or cling film for 10 minutes.  At 10 minutes, peel the
browned skin off and discard.  Cut chiles into 1-2 inch strips and set
aside.  Fry bacon bits till crisp, add minced garlic, chopped
scallions and corn.  Let it sizzle for about 3 mins.  Add salt and
pepper to taste. Toss shrimp only briefly till they start to look
opaque.  In a large casserole dish, layer the ingredients:  first the
rice, then the strips of poblano chiles, the tomatillas, chopped
cilantro, corn/bacon/garlic/shrimp mix and lastly the shredded
cheeses.  Bake for 30 minutes uncovered in middle of the oven.
Cheese should be browned when done.

Chef's Note:

This is a tasty, Mexican-styled, one dish meal, and is
excellent with black bean salsa!

# Truly Hearty Grits
## by Renate Sweat
### Phoenix

Yield:  8 portions
Preheat:  350°F

1 lb finely ground (raw) pork sausage or hamburger
1 clove garlic, minced or pressed
3/4 tsp pepper
1 tsp hot sauce
1 cup quick-cooking grits
2 tbsp butter or margarine
2 large eggs
2 cups shredded sharp cheddar cheese
1 fresh jalapeño, diced
1/3 cup fresh cilantro leaves

Crumble sausage or hamburger in skillet, brown about 6 minutes, drain, add garlic, pepper, hot sauce and diced fresh jalapeño. Set aside.

In a medium saucepan, boil grits with 4 cups water, simmer 5-6 minutes, add butter or margarine.

In a separate bowl, beat eggs to blend, then add cheese, meat mix, and grits.  Pour into lightly greased 9" x 13" baking dish.  Bake uncovered 45 minutes, let stand 5 minutes.  Garnish individual servings with roughly chopped cilantro.

Helpful Tips:

Always use gloves when cleaning or dicing fresh chiles.  To chop cilantro, first use kitchen scissors to snip off the leaves; discard stems, and then you can chop leaves more quickly.

# Vegetable Pie
## by Renate Sweat
## Phoenix

Yield:  4-6 portions
Preheat: 400°F

4-5 cups chopped fresh vegetables
2 tbsp minced onion
fresh or dried basil, parsely, and oregano
3/4 cup grated cheese (I like cheddar and parmesan)
1 1/2 cups Bisquick
1 1/2 cups milk
3 eggs
salt & pepper to taste
Optional:  1 cup chopped (cooked) chicken or ham.

Lightly grease a 9" x 13" baking dish.  Mix vegetables (and optional meat) with onion and herbs and put in dish.  Lay grated cheese on top.

Mix Bisquick, milk, eggs, salt and pepper until smooth; pour over cheese and vegetables.

Cover with foil and bake 30 minutes.  Remove foil and bake 15 minutes longer.  Serve hot; freshly sliced tomatoes with a light vinaigrette accompany this dish nicely.

# Hamburger Casserole
## by Rich and Claire Genser
## Tucson

Yield:  4-6 portions
Preheat:  350°F

1 lb hamburger
1 tbsp butter, margarine or olive oil
I can cream of mushroom soup
I can sliced mushrooms or 12 oz fresh, sautéed mushrooms
2 tbsp Worcestershire sauce
1 cup grated cheddar cheese
1 box Uncle Ben's wild rice (regular)

Brown hamburger in butter (etc) and set aside.  Cook wild rice according to instructions on box.  When both are done, place in casserole dish and add Worcestershire sauce, cheddar cheese, mushrooms, and mushroom soup.  Cover and bake for 30 minutes. This freezes very well and can be reheated in the microwave.

# Beer Stew
Mary Miller
Tempe

2-3 lbs beef stew meat, cut into bite-sized pieces
1 package oxtail soup mix
1 can beer

Put all ingredients into a crock pot on low all day.  Serve over rice or noodles and with a side dish of fresh, lightly-steamed vegetables in season.

*"Our lives are not in the lap of the gods, but in the lap of our cooks."*

Lin Yutang

# Crawfish Etouffée
## by Renée Guillory
## Phoenix

Yield: 8-10 portions

3 lbs uncooked crawfish (preserve fat)
4 1/2 sticks butter
4 onions, roughly chopped
4 medium green bell peppers, roughly chopped
8 stalks celery, roughly chopped
8 garlic cloves
1 cup parsely
6 tbsp Zatarain's seasoning (or the like)
1 can mushroom soup + 1 can water
1 can tomato paste + 1 can water
1 16 oz can diced, fireroasted tomatoes (I like Muir Glen)

Warm butter and garlic in large saucepan. Sauté onions till barely softened. Add remaining veggies, canned tomatoes, tomato paste, water, and mushroom soup. Mix well.

Add seasonings and stir for at least a minute. Add crawfish and fat, then turn heat to simmer (lower heat if the mixture bubbles). Heat uncovered 20-25 minutes; this is enough to cook the crawfish but keep the veggies firm. Stir at least twice during heating. Serve over rice and garnish with lots of parsely -- and keep the Tabasco handy.

Alternate preparation: For color and flavor variety, try different bell peppers till you suit your palate – keep at least one bell pepper green for the recipe, but with the three remaining needed, experiment with combinations of red, yellow, and orange, which are sweeter.

# Braising Greens with Pasta, Feta Cheese, and Toasted Pine Nuts
## by Boxed Greens*
## Tempe

Yield: 4-6 portions
Preheat: 350°F

2 cups braising greens, rinsed but not dried (baby spinach,
    arugula, dandelion, kale, chard, tango, or mustard)
1 lb tubular pasta or farfalle
3 oz feta cheese, crumbled
1/3 cup pine nuts
2 tbsp olive oil
2 fresh garlic cloves, sliced

Rinse braising greens and set aside. Spread pine nuts in single
layer on cookie sheet and brown about 10 minutes. Set aside to
cool. Fill large pot with water and begin heating to boil while
preparing greens.

In a large skillet, heat olive oil over medium-high heat and brown
garlic. Add greens and saute until wilted down; cover and turn off
heat. Cook pasta until al dente. When pasta is done, drain and
place in a large serving bowl. Sprinkle olive oil and mix to prevent
clumping. Stir greens and place greens on top of pasta. Sprinkle
with crumbled feta cheese and toasted pine nuts. Serve
immediately.

Variation: Add crushed red pepper flakes to greens when cooking
for spicier dish.

*Used with permission

# Green Chile Clam Chowder
## by Diane J. Brown
## Payson

Yield:  6-8 portions

4 large or 6 small red potatoes, peeled and diced
5-6 medium carrots, peeled and sliced
1 cup frozen corn
4 oz diced green chiles
2 pickled jalapeños, seeded and chopped
4 stalks celery, chopped
1/2 cup chopped onion
4 tbsp butter
28 oz chicken broth
2 cups half and half
1/2 cup cornstarch mixed with 1/2 cup water
20 oz chopped clams
salt and coarsely ground black pepper to taste
fresh, minced cilantro or parsely to garnish

Sauté onion, celery and jalapeño chiles in butter.  Add potatoes, carrots, corn, chiles, salt and pepper.  Mix well.  Then add chicken broth.  Simmer till vegetables are tender.  Mix in cornstarch and water.  When thickened, add clams and half and half.  Heat till hot, not boiling.  Tastes best the next day when flavors have had a chance to blend.  Before serving, sprinkle with minced cilantro or parsely.  Great with corn muffins or fry bread.


ONE FOR THE ROAD

My husband and I spend winters in Payson, Arizona, and summers in Eldora, Colorado.  On our way back and forth, we usually stop in Santa Fe, New Mexico, a town famous for its good food.  This soup is my successful try at replicating a delicious soup we ate in a Santa Fe restaurant.

# Wonderful Vegetarian Chili
## by Kathy Roediger
### Phoenix

Yield:  8-10 portions

Olive oil
2 medium zucchini, finely chopped
2 medium yellow onions, finely chopped
4 cloves garlic, minced
2 large sweet red peppers, cored and finely chopped
28 oz crushed tomatoes
14 oz stewed tomatoes
24 oz low-sodium vegetable juice
2 tbsp chili powder
1 tbsp ground cumin
1 tbsp dried basil
1 tbsp dried oregano
2 tbsp freshly ground black pepper
1 tsp salt
1 tsp fennel seeds
1/2 cup chopped Italian parsley or 1 cup dried parsley
1 cup each canned dark red kidney beans, pinto beans,
        garbanzo beans, and corn, drained and rinsed
1 tsp dill weed
2 tbsp lemon juice

Heat olive oil in a large skillet over medium heat. Add zucchini and
sauté until just tender. Remove zucchini to a large pot, straining
excess oil. Over low heat, into the skillet, add onions, garlic and red
pepper; sauté until just wilted, about 10 minutes.  Strain off excess
oil and add vegetables to the zucchini.  Place large pot over low
heat. Add crushed tomatoes, stewed tomatoes, vegetable juice,
chili powder, cumin, basil, oregano, black pepper, salt, fennel, and
parsley.  Simmer uncovered, stirring often, for 30 minutes. Stir in
kidney beans, pinto beans, garbanzo beans, corn, dill and lemon
juice.  Simmer another 15 minutes.  Stir well and adjust seasonings
to taste.  Serve immediately. Garnish with sliced scallions, grated
Colby-Jack cheese, and/or sour cream if desired.

# Beet and Fennel Soup
## by Boxed Greens*
## adapted by Renée Guillory
## Phoenix

Yield:   4 portions
Preheat:  400°F

6 medium beets
3 tbsp vegetable oil
3 large onions, sliced
1/4 tsp fennel seeds
3 fennel bulbs, sliced thinly, reserving leaves for garnish
2/3 cup water
3 cups chicken broth
4 tbsp fresh orange juice
fresh ground black pepper to taste

Trim beets, leaving 1 inch of stems attached, and scrub well.  Wrap beets tightly in foil and roast in middle of oven until tender, about 1 1/2 hours.  Unwrap beets carefully and let stand until cool.  Peel beets.  Cut half of 1 beet into very thin, 1-inch-long matchsticks for garnish and set aside.  Chop remaining beets.

In a large heavy saucepan, heat oil over medium heat until hot and cook onions with fennel seeds, stirring until softened, about 15 minutes.  Add sliced fennel and water and cook, covered, stirring frequently, until fennel is very soft.  Stir in chopped beets and broth and simmer uncovered about 15 minutes.  In a blender, puree soup in batches, transferring pureed batches to another saucepan over low heat.  Stir in orange juice and add pepper to taste.  Garnish soup with beet matchsticks and fennel leaves.  Serve with breadsticks.

*Used with permission

# Turkey Cutlets with Orange Sauce
## by Amy Kobeta
## Phoenix

Yield:  4 portions

2 tbsp all-purpose flour
salt & pepper to taste
1 lb turkey cutlets (boneless, skinless)
3 tbsp vegetable oil
1/3 cup sliced green onions, white part only
1 tbsp finely sliced green onion tops
1 garlic clove, thinly sliced
1 1/2 cups fresh or frozen orange juice
3 tbsp soy vey sauce
12 oz wide egg noodles

Combine flour with salt & pepper.  Lightly cover turkey cutlets with flour, shaking off excess.  Heat oil in large skillet over medium high heat.  Add cutlets and cook until browned, about 7 minutes on each side (less for thinly-sliced cutlets).

Begin preparing noodles according to instructions.

Lower heat in skillet to simmer.  Transfer turkey to a plate and set aside.  In the skillet, add green onion bottoms and tops, garlic, and stir frequently just until softened, about 30 seconds.

Add orange juice and soy vey and bring to a light boil.  Stir often, making sure to scrape the pan and incorporate all drippings and vegetables into sauce.  Heat sauce until juice reduces and thickens.  Return turkey to the skillet and baste  with the sauce.  Heat together, uncovered, for 5 minutes; lower heat if necessary.

Serve turkey over the noodles and drizzle remaining sauce over the portions. A green, slightly bitter salad (think about mixing in some arugula or endive) and light vinaigrette complements this main course well.  Enjoy!

# More Wonderful Vegetarian Chili
## by Renée Guillory
## Phoenix

Yield:  8-10 portions

3 tbsp cooking oil
3 medium onions, chopped
1 medium green pepper, chopped
1 medium red pepper, chopped
1 fresh salad tomato, chopped with pulp and seeds
2 stalks celery, chopped
4 cloves garlic, minced or pressed
3 fresh jalapeño chiles, minced
28 oz can stewed tomatoes + 1 can water
16 oz each kidney beans, cannellini beans, black beans, and pinto
        beans, drained
1/2 tsp oregano flakes
1 tsp cumin
1 tbsp + 1 tsp chili powder
1 1/2 tsp freshly ground black pepper
salt to taste

Garnishes:
1 cup freshly chopped cilantro
1 cup plain yogurt or sour cream
1 cup shredded Monterey Jack or sharp cheddar cheese

In a large stew pot, heat the oil.  Add onions, peppers, celery, and
garlic.  Heat just until tender, stirring constantly.  Add the fresh and
canned tomatoes and all spices except salt.  Simmer 20 minutes
while you prepare the garnishes for the table.  Add the beans and
jalapeños and simmer for another 20 minutes, then taste and add
salt.  Serve with warm tortillas.

# Shiitake Mushrooms
# and Chicken Tetrazzini
by Boxed Greens*
Tempe

Yield: 4 portions
Preheat: 375°F

6 oz dried spaghetti
1 1/2 tbsp cornstarch
1 1/2 cups nonfat evaporated milk
1 cup canned nonfat reduced sodium chicken broth
1/4 tsp ground pepper
4 oz shiitake mushrooms, thinly sliced
1 carrot, grated
1/6 cup dry sherry
1/16 tsp ground nutmeg
several drops hot pepper sauce
1 1/2 cups cooked, diced chicken breast meat
1/8 cup whole wheat bread crumbs
1 1/2 tbsp grated Parmesan cheese

Bring a large pot of water to boiling and cook pasta until al dente.
While pasta cooks, coat a 2-quart baking dish with nonstick
cooking spray. In a large saucepan over medium-high heat, whisk
the cornstarch and evaporated milk until blended. Add the
chicken broth and pepper and bring to a boil, reduce heat to low
and simmer, whisking frequently until the sauce has thickened
slightly, about 5 minutes. Stir in mushrooms and carrot and cover
and simmer until tender. Stir in sherry, nutmeg, pepper sauce and
chicken. Drain the pasta and put in prepared baking dish. Add
sauce and combine. Sprinkle with bread crumbs and cheese.

Bake until the topping is lightly browned and sauce is bubbling,
about 20 minutes.

* Used with permission

# Quick Alfredo Pasta Sauce
## by Rich and Claire Genser
## Tucson

Yield:  4 portions

2 tbsp butter or margarine
dash white pepper
2 tbsp flour
1 cup milk (even 1% will do)
1/2 cup parmesan cheese

Melt butter; add dash of white pepper and flour and whisk until bubbly. Slowly add milk and whisk until smooth over medium heat. Reduce heat to simmer and add parmesan cheese.  Whisk until smooth. Cover and remove from heat until ready to serve.  This is great over spinach noodles or any pasta.  Before serving, reheat on low.

# Fresh Mushroom Pasta Sauce
## by Bertha Cook
## Cornville

1 1/2 lbs fresh mushrooms, brushed then sliced thinly
1 clove garlic, minced or pressed
1 tsp salt
fresh ground pepper
1/2 cup olive oil
1/4 cup butter
2 1/2 cup canned tomatoes
1/2 tsp oregano

Simmer mushrooms, garlic, salt and pepper in combined olive oil and butter for 10 minutes, stirring frequently.  Add tomatoes and oregano and simmer for 30 minutes.  Serve over hot pasta.

# Sunflower Seed Pasta Sauce
by Bertha Cook
Cornville

Yield: 4 portions

1 1/2 cups parsely
1/4 cup olive oil
1 tsp dry basil (or 1 tbsp chopped fresh basil)
1 1/2 cloves garlic, minced or pressed
1/8 tsp salt

Place the above ingredients in a blender and blend until mixture is emulsified.

Stir in:
1/2 cup unsalted sunflower seeds
1/4 cup Parmesan cheese, grated

Mix into 1/2 lb. piping hot pasta. Serve and enjoy immediately.

# Whole-Wheat Spaghetti with Arugula, Walnuts and Pecorino
## by Boxed Greens*
## Tempe

Yield: 4-6 portions

1 lb whole wheat spaghetti
salt
4 tbsp olive oil, plus extra to finish
3 garlic cloves, chopped
several pinches of crushed red pepper flakes
6 cups arugula, coarsely chopped
3 tbsp chopped parsely
freshly grated pecorino
1/2 cup chopped walnuts

Drop pasta in salted boiling water and cook until al dente. Meanwhile, heat oil in large skillet and add garlic and chile and cook over medium heat until garlic turns light gold. Add arugula, season with a few pinches of salt and saute until wilted. Stir in parsely and turn off heat.

When pasta is done, scoop out and add directly to pan. Toss well and add walnuts, toss again and serve with a dusting of cheese on top and extra virgin olive oil drizzled over the top.

*Used with permission

# Buckwheat Pancakes
## by Jim McCarthy
## Flagstaff

1 cup white flour
1 cup buckwheat flour
1 tsp baking soda
1 tbsp baking powder
1/2 tsp salt
2 tsp sugar

Mix above dry ingredients together, then add:

2 beaten eggs
1/4 cup cooking oil
2 cups milk
blueberries (if frozen, defrost first)

Using a quarter-cup measuring cup, spoon the resulting batter onto greased griddle (I use solid vegetable shortening) heated to approximately 360°F. Pancakes will bubble when they are ready to be turned; turn pancakes only once.

Chef's Note:

These hearty pancakes are a treat worthy of center stage at any breakfast celebration. Enjoy!

# Food for Outings

Family camping is back in vogue – not that it ever really went out of style. The following recipes have been developed by seasoned outings chefs. Most are quite humble (and simple to reproduce) while some require more planning and preparation time. All of these tried and true trail recipes are especially suited for large groups. In many cases, recipes are fairly easily divided, and some even include instructions for smaller portions for your convenience.

Please remember to obey fire safety rules and common sense when cooking outdoors. Always check for fire restrictions before planning elaborate meals on your next camping trip or backpacking venture. And if there is a green light for outdoor cooking, follow the guidelines established by the agency responsible for the public lands you're visiting.

Many of these outings recipes include dried foods to reduce traveling weight and for fool-proof storage until food is cooked. Naturally, if you have the inclination, you can experiment with fresh foods substituted for the freeze dried. Two things to keep in mind: you will need to reduce the water called for in a recipe since you're not reconstituting dried foods; and you may need to play with the order in which the vegetables are added, so as not to overcook them.

If you're substituting fresh for freeze-dried foods, I recommend experimenting in the kitchen to perfect the dish – just go crazy. This way, there's no disappointment in the great outdoors. After all, your meals on the trail should be savored!

      – R.H.G.

# Piroque Jambalaya
## by Chris Trask
## Tempe


1 tbsp cajun seasoning
1 tsp onion flakes
1/8 tsp garlic flakes
1 tsp green pepper flakes
1 tsp celery flakes
1 tsp parsley flakes
1 tsp dried chives
1/2 cup freeze-dried green beans
1/2 cup freeze-dried peas


Seal all of the above ingredients in a labeled pouch for easy travel storage.

To prepare, empty the pouch into 3 cups boiling water; reduce heat and let simmer for 5 minutes. Add 1 cup minute rice, stir, cover, and remove from heat. Let steep for 5 minutes.

# Canoe Stew
## by Chris Trask
## Tempe

Seal these ingredients in a labeled pouch:

3⁄4 cup freeze-dried green beans
3⁄4 cup freeze-dried peas
1 tsp onion flakes
2 tsp dill weed

- - - - - - - - - - - -
Have on hand:

1 pkg (3⁄4 oz) brown gravy mix
1/2 tsp salt
- - - - - - - - - - - -

Seal these ingredients in a separate labeled pouch:
1 pkg (2 oz) instant mashed potatoes
1⁄2 tsp salt
1/2 pkg (1/4 oz) butter buds
1 1⁄2 tbsp powdered milk

To prepare, empty the vegetable and herb ingredients from the storage pouch into a pot with 1 cup of water and bring to a boil. Turn down the heat and simmer for an additional 5 minutes, then add the gravy mix and stir. Continue simmering until the sauce thickens. Meanwhile, put 1 1/2 cups of water and 1/2 tsp salt into another pot and bring to a boil. Add the mashed potato ingredients and stir until they are the right consistency. Serve the vegetable mix over the mashed potatoes.

# Zucchini al Pomodori Secco
## by Chris Trask
## Tempe

5 tbsp tomato flakes
1/8 tsp basil
1/2 small bay leaf
1/8 tsp marjoram
1/8 tsp oregano
2 cup sliced zucchini
1/2 cup dried mushrooms
1/4 tsp garlic flakes
1 tsp onion flakes
2 tsp parsley flakes

Place the tomato flakes, basil, bay leaf, marjoram, and oregano in a blender and process until reduced to a fine powder. Place in a sealed and labeled pouch with the other ingredients for easy travel storage.

To prepare, empty the pouch into a pot with 2 cups of water. Bring to a boil; reduce heat and simmer, stirring occasionally, for 5 minutes longer.  Add a package of Ramen noodles, stir to moisten, and simmer for 5 minutes longer.

# Vegetables aux Herbes Secher
## by Chris Trask
## Tempe

5 tbsp tomato flakes
1/4 tsp basil
1/4 tsp oregano
1/8 tsp tarragon
1/4 tsp chervil
1/4 tsp sage
1 tsp dried chives
2 cup dried mushrooms
1/2 cup freeze-dried green beans
1/2 cup freeze-dried peas

Place the tomato flakes, basil, oregano, tarragon, chervil, and sage in a blender and process until reduced to a fine powder. Place in a sealed, labeled pouch with the other ingredients for easy travel storage.

To prepare, place in a pot with 2 cups of water.  Bring to a boil; reduce heat and simmer, stirring occasionally, for 5 minutes longer. Add a package of Ramen noodles, stir to moisten, and simmer for 5 minutes longer.

# Murry Curry
## by Chris Trask
Tempe

1 tbsp Curry powder
1/4 tsp garlic flakes
1 tsp parsley flakes
1/8 tsp tarragon
3/4 cup freeze-dried green beans
3/4 cup freeze-dried peas

Place all of these ingredients in a sealed, labeled pouch for easy travel storage.

To prepare, empty pouch into a pot with 3 cups of water. Bring to a boil; reduce heat and simmer, stirring occasionally, for 5 minutes longer. Stir in 1 cup of minute rice, stir to moisten, cover, and let steep for 5 minutes longer.

# Pesto and Pine Nut Linguine
## by Doug Pilcher
## Phoenix

Yield:  20 portions

4 lbs linguine
10 oz Pesto, pre mixed bottle
12 oz Reggiano parmesan cheese, finely grated
8 yellow squash, julienne
4 zucchini, julienne
2 red bell peppers, julienne
12 oz pine nuts
2 cloves garlic, minced
black pepper
butter

Place a large pot of water on the stove and bring to boil.  In the meantime, finely grate parmesan cheese and set aside.  Julienne yellow squash, zucchini and red bell pepper and place in a medium bowl with pine nuts, garlic and black pepper.  Once the water begins to boil add a shot of olive oil and stir in the pasta.  At the same time heat butter in a medium skillet or wok and sauté the veggie mixture.

Drain the pasta and quickly rinse with cold clean water.  Place pasta in a large bowl and mix in pesto and half of cheese.  Serve pasta topped with sautéed veggies and remaining cheese with beer bread on the side.

# Moroccan Stew with Couscous
## by Doug Pilcher
## Phoenix

Yield: 20 portions

6 1/4  cups red wine
7 1/2  cups tomato sauce
1 1/8  tbsp allspice
1 1/8  tbsp basil
1 3/4  tsp cayenne
1 3/4  tsp ground cumin
1 1/8  tsp curry powder
1 1/2  tsp salt
15 cloves garlic
7 1/2  red onions, sliced
4  green bell peppers, sliced
1 1/4  stalks celery, chopped
1 1/4  lbs mushrooms, sliced
5 carrots, sliced
2 lbs garbanzo beans, canned
1 1/2  cups walnut pieces
3  10 oz cans chicken
--------------------------------
8  cups couscous
10  cups water
6  veggie bouillon cubes
1  cup olive oil
2  tsp salt

In a medium pot add wine, tomato sauce, spices and garlic.
Simmer for one hour or until sauce thickens. In a large wok or
skillet, sauté vegetables in a small amount of olive oil. As
vegetables near completion, stir in 1/2 of sauce. Serve over
steaming couscous with extra sauce on the side and optional
chicken for meat lovers. In a large pot bring water, bouillon, oil
and salt to a boil. Add couscous and bring to a boil. Remove from
heat, cover and let stand for 5 minutes. Fluff with a fork and serve.
In a small skillet, sauté chicken in basil and olive oil.

# Hearty Lentil Mushroom Soup
## by Doug Pilcher
## Phoenix

Yield:  20 portions

3 1/3  cups dried lentils
4 russet potatoes, cubed
1/3 cup oil
4 garlic cloves, minced
3 yellow onions, sliced
4 veggie bouillon cubes
4 14 oz. cans stewed tomatoes, regular, undrained
2 lbs mushrooms, sliced
5 carrots, thinly sliced
1 stalk celery, chopped
4 tbsp Worcestershire sauce
3 tbsp vinegar
1/2 tsp crushed red pepper
1/4 cup dried parsley
1/2 tsp black pepper
1 tsp salt

In the morning, cover lentils and potatoes with water and boil for 1 hour.  Allow lentils and potatoes to rest in the water.

In the afternoon, drain and separate lentils and potatoes.  In a large pot, cover lentils with water and boil for 1 hour.  In a skillet, heat oil and sauté garlic and onion.  Rinse and drain lentils.  Put lentils back into large pot and add the veggie bouillon cubes, fresh water and tomatoes.  Cover and simmer 45 minutes.  Add the boiled potatoes, mushrooms, carrots, celery, Worcestershire sauce, vinegar, red pepper, parsley, black pepper and salt.  Cover and simmer 60 minutes or until lentils and vegetables are tender.

# Tuscan Stew
by Doug Pilcher
Phoenix

Yield: 20 portions

2 yellow onions, chopped
4 sprigs celery, thin sliced
4 16 oz cans Great Northern beans, drained
4 14 oz cans stewed tomatoes
4 26 oz jars spaghetti sauce
1/2  tsp crushed red pepper
black pepper
1 1/2  lbs bow tie pasta
1 lb mozzarella cheese, grated

In a large pot, sauté onions and celery in small amount of oil.  Add
beans, tomatoes, spaghetti sauce, red pepper, black pepper (to
taste) and simmer.  Cook and drain pasta, then add to sauce.  Top
servings with mozzarella cheese.

# Lizard Head Lasagna
# Dutch Oven Dinner
by Doug Pilcher
Phoenix

Yield: 20 portions

3 lbs lasagna noodles
3 yellow onions, chopped
2 green bell peppers, sliced
20  garlic cloves, minced
3 tbsp olive oil
3 lbs mushrooms, sliced
3 lbs spinach, canned
2 tsp salt
2 tsp black pepper
1 tsp nutmeg
5  eggs
4 lbs ricotta cheese
1  No. 10 can spaghetti sauce
3 lbs mozzarella cheese, sliced
Parmesan cheese

Fire up approximately 60 coals. Cook lasagna noodles, drain and set aside. Sauté onion, bell pepper and garlic in oil. Lower heat and add the mushrooms; cook until almost all the liquid has evaporated. Add spinach. Increase heat and stir until almost all liquid has cooked away. Add salt, pepper and nutmeg. Set the mixture aside. Stir the egg into ricotta and set aside.

To assemble, coat the Dutch Ovens with oil. Spread half the tomato sauce onto the bottom of the Dutch ovens. Lay one-third of the pasta over the tomato sauce. Spread half the ricotta over the pasta and then half the spinach mixture over the ricotta. Add 1/3 of the mozzarella slices. Cover with another layer of pasta and then repeat ricotta, spinach and mozzarella layers. Lay the remaining pasta on top. Spread the rest of the tomato sauce over the pasta and add slices of mozzarella on top of the lasagna. Bake 60 minutes over a 20/10 setup of coals (20 coals on top, 10 below the oven to ensure even cooking).

Serve with parmesan cheese.


Chef's Note:

This recipe was named after Lizard Head Wilderness in Colorado where it was perfected on a service trip.

# Red Sonoran Enchiladas
# Dutch Oven Dinner
by Doug Pilcher
Phoenix

Yield: 20 portions

2  21 oz cans enchilada sauce
2  21 oz cans red chili sauce
1 lb green chiles, sliced
8 oz black olives, sliced
3 yellow onions, chopped
4 lbs cheese, grated
70 corn tortillas
3 10 oz. cans chicken
1 lg can jalapeño, whole
1 head lettuce, chopped
4 tomatoes, chopped

Fire up approximately 60 coals.

Use two Dutch Ovens, one for veggie and one for chicken enchiladas. Coat the bottom of each Dutch Oven with a little oil, then red chili sauce.  Spread eight corn tortillas evenly across the bottom.  Follow with sprinkles of chiles, onions, cheese, sauce, (and chicken to one oven.)  Continue with another layer of corn tortillas and ingredients until all stuff is used.  Place any remaining ingredients, including the black olives, some cheese and sauce on top of the pile, put the lids on and cook for 45 minutes over a 20/10 setup of coals (20 coals on top of the oven, 10 below it – this ensures even cooking).  Serve with whole jalapeños, lettuce, and tomatoes on the side.

# Chiles Rellenos Dutch Oven Dinner
## by Doug Pilcher
### Phoenix

Yield:  20 portions

3 lbs whole green chiles
4 lbs cheddar cheese, grated
18 eggs
4 cups milk
1 lb black olives, sliced
2  cups tomato sauce
5 cups Bisquick
1 1/2  tsp salt
3  10 oz cans chicken
salsa

Fire up about 60 coals.  Lightly oil two Dutch Ovens, one for veggie chiles rellenos and one for chicken chiles rellenos.  Split open chiles and arrange in the bottom of each oven.  Cover with cheese. Blend eggs, salt, olives, milk and Bisquick.  Pour over cheese. Gently mix chicken into only one of the ovens.  Bake 60 minutes with a 20/10 setup of coals (20 coals on top of the oven, 10 below it – this ensures even cooking).  Serve with salsa.

# Huevos Mountainadas
# Dutch Oven Breakfast
by Doug Pilcher
Phoenix

Yield: 20 portions

8 russet potatoes, cooked the night before and cubed
20 eggs
8 cups milk
4 tsp salt
4 tsp black pepper
1 tsp dry mustard
4 tsp Louisiana hot sauce
18 slices whole wheat bread
2 lbs cheddar cheese, grated
3 4 oz cans green chiles, diced
2 yellow onions, chopped
1 2 lb ham, diced (optional)

The night before, boil potatoes until tender but firm, drain and set aside.

In the morning, cut up potatoes into 1/2" cubes and prepare other ingredients. In a large bowl, mix eggs with milk and add salt, pepper, dry mustard and hot sauce. Beat eggs thoroughly. Add chiles, onions and potatoes. Add bread, cut in 1" cubes, and add 75% of cheese. Lightly oil two Dutch Ovens and equally divide the mixture in the ovens. Sprinkle the remaining cheese on top, put on the lid and cook 45 minutes or until eggs are firm over a 14/10 setup of coals (14 coals on top of the oven, 10 below it – this ensures even cooking).

# Greek Chicken
## by Edith Reeves and John Ricker
## Phoenix

Yield: 20 portions

5  3 lb chickens, cut up and skinned (debone if you prefer)
salt & pepper to taste
8 tbsp dried oregano
3 tbsp butter or margarine
1 large head garlic, sliced
2 1/2 cups lemon juice

Heat a Dutch Oven over medium heat, and put the butter or margarine in the bottom, making sure that the bottom is covered completely.  Place chicken pieces in the dutch oven and sprinkle in the spices and garlic.  Add about 1 cup of the lemon juice, setting the rest aside.  As chicken cooks, baste often and gradually add the remaining lemon juice.  Chicken will take about 45 minutes to cook.

Prepare the rice, following instructions for 32 ounces of rice, except you must subtract 5 minutes from cooking time.

When chicken is cooked, remove cooked chicken to another pot. Reserve and defat the broth that is in the Dutch Oven.  Add the almost-cooked rice to the Dutch Oven with the broth – fluff the rice into the broth and spices and cook for five minutes.  Serve the chicken over the savory rice.

# Chicken with Peaches & Walnuts
## by Edith Reeves
## Phoenix

| Yield: | 5 | 8 | 15 |
|---|---|---|---|
| **Ingredients:** | | | |
| Chicken soup mix, packages | 1 | 3 | 4 |
| Walnuts | 1/2 cup | 1 3/4 cups | 2 1/2 cups |
| Dried peaches | 3 oz | 6 oz | 9 oz |
| Powdered milk | 1/3 cup | 1 1/2 cups | 2 cups |
| Freeze-dried chicken | 4 oz | 8 oz | 16 oz |
| Butter | 2 tbsp | 4 oz | 8 oz |
| Water | 1 3/4 cups | 3 cups | 4 1/2 cups |
| Sherry | 2 tbsp | 1/3 cup | 1/2 cup |

Prepare rice. Place all ingredients except sherry in required amount of water and cook 15 minutes until thickened. Just before serving, add the sherry. Serve over hot rice.

# Yams with Ham, Apples, and Carrots
## by Edith Reeves
### Phoenix

| Yield: | 5 | 8 | 15 |
|---|---|---|---|
| **Ingredients:** | | | |
| Ham, diced (inches) | 5 in | 8 in | 15 in |
| Dried apples, diced | 4 oz | 6 oz | 12 oz |
| Dried carrots | 1 1/2 oz | 3 oz | 5 oz |
| Orange peel | 1 tsp | 1 1/2 tsp | 2 1/2 tsp |
| Butter | 1/4 cup | 3/4 cup | 1 1/4 cups |
| Yams, freeze-dried | 7 oz | 11 oz | 22 oz |
| Brown sugar | 3 tbsp | 5 tbsp | 10 tbsp |
| Water | 1 3/4 cups | 3 cups | 6 cups |

Boil slightly more water than the recipe calls for. Place the yams and carrots into the pot you will use to prepare the casserole. Slowly add boiling water to yams and carrots – you may need slightly more or less water to reconstitute them to the proper consistency. Once these vegetables are reconstituted, add all remaining ingredients and mix well. Heat and serve.

# Rocky Mountain Mud
## by Doug Pilcher
Phoenix

Yield:  20 portions

8 cups graham cracker crumbs
2 cups pecans, chopped
1 cup powdered sugar
20 oz semisweet chocolate
1 1/3  cups whole powdered milk
1 3/4  cups water
2 tsp vanilla
powdered sugar

Premix crumbs, sugar and pecans.  Add 1 cup water to milk powder. Heat, add chocolate, and stir until melted.  Add remaining ingredients.  Mix well, press into pan.  Sprinkle a little powdered sugar on top and place in a cool location to stand for at least two hours before serving.

# Trail Mix
## by Dean Guillory
### Surprise

3 cups nuts (almonds, peanuts, cashews)
1 cup roasted soybeans or roasted sunflower seeds
2 cups dried fruit (raisins, cranberries, cherries)
2 cups granola
one large package of M & M's (peanut or plain)

Mix and store in airtight container.

Chef's Note:

Our family and camping buddies know from experience that 8 hikers can snack this tasty trail mix away to nothing over a long weekend.  Enjoy!

## "Food is an important part of a balanced diet."

Fran Lebowitz

# Civil War Cake
## by Edith Reeves
### Phoenix

Preheat: 375°F

Boil 5 minutes, strain raisins, and let cool (reserve water):
1 lb raisins
2 cups sugar
2 cups water

Mix together:
3 cups all-purpose flour
1 tsp cinnamon
1 tsp cloves
1 tsp salt
1/2 tsp nutmeg

Have on hand:
1 tsp baking soda
2 8"x4" cake pans, greased and floured

Add the cooled raisins to the flour mix and mix well. Warm the raisin water again and use about 2 tsp. to mix with the baking soda. Put the baking soda mixture into the flour and raisin mixture and stir thoroughly. Pour resulting batter into two 8" x 4" greased and floured cake pans. Bake one hour; let stand 5 minutes then turn out onto cooling rack.

Chef's Note:

This recipe dates from the Civil War era. At that time, eggs, milk, and butter were hard to come by. The modern benefit to this is that the cake has no cholesterol and is vegan. It's a great treat for the trail – even for week-long backpacking trips. At home, it could last for weeks (but never does, it's eaten too quickly) wrapped in plastic or stored in an airtight container.

The Civil War Cake recipe was given to my family by Grace Gemunden, a Southern Georgia gal. During the Civil War, at only 13 years of age, Grace came home from school one day and her mother told her to go to her bedroom and put on the clothes lying on her bed. She obeyed, came downstairs in a white dress, and was married off to a 40-year-old Colonel in the Confederate army. He didn't survive the war and later Grace married George Gemunden. Grace and George moved to Philadelphia and rented two rooms from my parents. They became surrogate grandparents to my two brothers and myself. We called them "Tata" and "Uncle." Tata lived until the age of 93 and always remained our close family friend.

# Beverages

# Spicy Lemonade
## by Mary Miller
### Tempe

4 cups water
1 cup sugar
10 whole cloves
10 whole allspice
2 cinnamon sticks
2 1/2 cups crushed ice
1 cup fresh lemon juice

Combine water, sugar & spices in sauce pan and bring mixture to a boil. Lower heat and simmer uncovered for 5 minutes. Remove spices and discard.

Pour into 2 quart picture and chill. Add ice & lemon juice to pitcher and serve.

# Spiced Tea
## by Bertha Cook
### Cornville

6 black teabags
1/4 tsp nutmeg
1/4 tsp allspice
1/4 tsp cinnamon
2 1/2 cups boiling water
3/4 cup granulated sugar
1/2 cup orange juice
1/3 cup lemon juice
2 cups cranberry juice
1 1/2 cups cold water

Boil water in kettle. Place teabags and spices in a saucepan, and pour boiling water over them. Let steep 3 minutes. Strain through a clean cloth, add sugar and let cool. Pour into pitcher. Add fruit juices and water. Pour into glasses over ice cubes and serve.

# Amy's Iced Tea
by Amy Kobeta
Phoenix, AZ


1 quart water
1/4 cup sugar
2 herbal tea bags (best with Celestial Seasonings strawberry kiwi or
mixed berry)
3 decaf black tea bags (or one family-sized bag)
Ice


Bring water to boil in saucepan. Turn off heat. Add sugar, herbal
tea bags, and black tea bags. Stir just until sugar dissolves and tea
bags are soaked. Let steep 5 minutes. Remove bags and pour
into 2 quart pitcher filled about halfway with ice. Serve chilled.

*"Some say the glass is
half empty, some say
the glass is half full.
I say, 'Are you going
to drink that?'"*

Lisa Claymen

# Wine:  An Ideal Accompaniment For Food
## by John Vankat*

Most wine reviews read something like this: "Tannic, but with lots of flesh and muscular currant, cassis, iron, and dark chocolate notes."  These can be fun to read, but I suspect most wine drinkers either disregard such verbiage or, worse yet, feel inadequate when they can't identify these flavors in wine. Moreover, these wine reviews falsely imply that wine tasting is a precise science.

The best way to dramatically increase your understanding and enjoyment of wine is to set the flowery prose aside and get back to basics. So pour yourself a glass and read on.

First Sip

Take that first sip, slosh it around your mouth, and focus on the wine's body and intensity. Body refers to the physical texture or feel (not taste) of the wine in your mouth and is especially easy to perceive on the top of your tongue. Wines range from watery ("thin" or "light-bodied") to somewhat syrupy ("heavy" or "full-bodied").

Intensity is the strength of the flavors, with wines ranging from "light" to "bold" or "flavorful." Intensity helps you decide what food to pair with the wine, because the wine should be more flavorful than the food.

Second Sip

Next, determine the balance of the wine. Balance is your perception of the relative strengths of sweetness, acidity, alcohol and, in red wines, astringency.

Sweetness, of course, is the most familiar taste. All wines have sugars, and when these dominate other flavors, the wine is "sweet". When other flavors mask the sugars, the wine is "dry".

- - - - - - - - - - - - - - - - - - -
* John Vankat is the wine columnist for the *Arizona Daily Sun* and can be reached at azpinewine@yahoo.com.

Acidity can hide sweetness, as it does in green apples. Many people perceive acidity best on the sides of their tongue. Over-acidic wines are "acidic" or "tart," well-balanced wines are "crisp" or "fresh" and under-acidic wines are "flat" or "flabby" because they lack pizzazz.

Alcohol also can mask other flavors. If it is excessive, the wine seems warm and is described as "hot." Astringency comes from tannins and can dominate red wines. It is sensed as a fuzzy coating on your teeth. Overly "tannic" wines taste coarse or rough, but tannins can make wine more age worthy.

Different wines are successful with different blends of these tastes. Such wines are "well-balanced." If one of the components is overemphasized, the wine is "unbalanced."

## Third Sip

Next, note the specific taste components, but forget about identifying the multitude of flavors. Focus on fruit and oak instead. Fruit flavors depend on how well flavors of the grapes show up in the finished wine. Oak flavors are imparted to wine from barrels during fermentation and aging. Individual wine drinkers have preferences for or against "fruity" and "oaky" wines.

## Fourth Sip

Swallow and note how the flavors finish in your mouth. Finish refers to the length and quality of the taste after swallowing. Terms for length range from "short" (gone in a few seconds) to "lingering" (lasting 60 seconds or more) Of course, the best wines have a long, pleasant finish.

## Later

Practice this basic approach to tasting wines and soon you'll be able to state what styles of wine you prefer. Instead of asking for "a good sauvignon blanc" when shopping or dining out, you'll be able to request "a crisp, medium-bodied, boldly flavored sauvignon blanc." Your level of confidence about wine will dramatically increase, as will your skill at selecting wines you like and selecting wine and food pairings that please your palate.

# Pairing Wine With Food

Part of the reason mystery surrounds this topic is that there are innumerable wine and food combinations.

Another reason is the illusion that every meal has an exact wine match. This idea is promulgated by magazine articles listing specific wines for specific menus and by books promising to help find "the perfect wine."

Principles

At the core of successfully pairing wine with food are three simple ideas.

First, select wine with a flavor intensity that is close to the intensity of the food. As you become skilled at this, you'll learn that by selecting wine that is somewhat more flavorful than the food, the wine becomes the primary focus of the meal. By selecting wine that is less flavorful than the food, the wine becomes secondary. And don't forget to adjust for spices and sauces. For example, I like chardonnay with salmon, but when my wife adds chili pepper rub to the salmon (a surprisingly wonderful combination), pinot noir is a much better choice.

Second, select wine with similar complexity and refinement as the food. A simple table wine is great with casual food such as meatloaf, while a more complex wine pairs best with more complex food.

Third, experiment with different pairings. Focusing on similarities between wine and food usually works, but contrasts are always interesting and sometimes surprisingly enjoyable. For instance, a full-bodied, buttery chardonnay would seem to be a good match for pasta and white sauce, but a lean, crisp white wine provides a tasty contrast with this creamy dish. By the way, an inexpensive way to experiment with different pairings is to always leave a little wine in the bottle to sip with tomorrow's dinner.

Wine Intensities

A list of wines in order of flavor intensity is a starting point for developing pairings:

Light Whites:  chenin blanc
Medium Whites:  riesling, pinot gris/grigio, sauvignon
           blanc, viognier
Strong Whites:  chardonnay, pinot blanc, semillon,
           gewürztraminer
Rosés and Light Reds:  rosé, gamay, grenache
Medium Reds:  sangiovese, pinot noir, merlot
Strong Reds:  shiraz (syrah), zinfandel, cabernet sauvignon

For example, if you're roasting pork without spices or sauce, pair this moderately flavorful meat with wines in the middle of the list, that is, medium whites to medium reds.  To focus on the pork, serve a wine toward the lighter end of this range, such as riesling.  To highlight the wine, go with something from the stronger end, such as merlot.

Favorite Pairings

As you experiment, you'll develop favorite wine and food pairings.  Here are a few of mine:

Riesling with ham
Sauvignon blanc with salad and veggies
Gewürztraminer with turkey
Gamay with hamburgers and pizza
Pinot noir with lamb
Shiraz and zinfandel with barbeque ribs
Zinfandel with red sauced pasta
Cabernet sauvignon with grilled steak

Of course, the best part of finding your own favorite pairings is that the process is so enjoyable!

*"A man who was fond of wine was offered some grapes at dessert after dinner. 'Much obliged,' said he, pushing the plate aside; 'I am not accustomed to take my wine in pills.'"*

Jean Anthelme Brillat-Savarin

# Desserts

# Alice's Cheesecake
## by Jean Berringer
## Phoenix

Preheat: 300°F

crust:
1/2 lb soft margarine
6 tbsp sugar
2 eggs
2 cups flour
1 tsp baking powder
cinnamon

Combine all these ingredients except cinnamon, making a batter. Grease a 15"x9-1/2" pan. With floured hands, press batter along the sides and bottom of pan, making a thin layer. Sprinkle the crust with cinnamon.

filling:
1 lb cream cheese or creamed cottage cheese
1 1/2 cups sugar
1/2 pint sour cream
6 whole eggs
2 tbsp flour
1 tsp vanilla
1 1/2 cups milk

Cream sugar and cheese together. Add eggs singly, blending each woll. In a separate bowl, blend flour with milk, then add the vanilla. Combine with cheese mixture. Mix well and pour into crust. Bake 1 hour and 10 minutes.

# Brigadeiros
by Denise Berringer-Wood
Phoenix

1 can Nestle La Lechera sweetened condensed milk (in the
        Mexican foods aisle, usually)
2 heaping tbsp cocoa mix
1/2 tbsp baking cocoa
2 tbsp butter
1 big container chocolate or rainbow sprinkles
1-2 plastic sandwich bags

Pour condensed milk into a small heavy-bottomed saucepan. Stir in cocoas and butter under medium-low heat. Stir constantly (about 30 minutes) until thickened enough that when stirred slowly, the bottom of the pan remains visible. Allow to cool completely. Once your pan is cool to the touch, you can spread the mixture around the sides of your pan and refrigerate to speed the process along. When it's ready, use your sandwich bags as gloves to roll the mixture into balls (it's very sticky). Roll the balls in the candy sprinkles and place on a plate. Keep chilled until ready to serve.

A SWEET ADDICTION

These awesome, chocolaty soft caramel Brazilian treats are ubiquitous down there, and for good reason. They take a lot of patience to make, so be prepared. Our study abroad group had to have them almost daily – sometimes they were available rolled racquetball-sized. They're great to make (a bit smaller) for parties or potlucks.

# Irish Cream Fudge
by Bertha Cook
Cornville

Yield: 16 servings

1 1/2 cups sugar
2/3 cup Irish Creme liqueur
1/4 cup butter or margarine
1 1/2 cups white chocolate chips
1 tsp vanilla

Mix Irish Creme and sugar in a 3 quart sauce pan. Add butter and bring to a boil, stirring constantly. Boil 5 minutes. Remove from heat. Add chips and vanilla. Stir, then whisk until chips melt and mixture is smooth. Spread into a wax-lined, 8" square pan. Chill 6 hours. Remove fudge from pan, cut into 2" squares, and enjoy.

# Timp Point Tira Misu
## by Sharon Galbreath
## Flagstaff

Yield: 8 portions

500 gram tub of mascarpone cheese
1 cup heavy cream (organic would be best)
1/4 cup sugar
1 tsp vanilla
2 tsp of espresso powder & 6 ounces of hot water combined
1/4 cup of dark rum
1/2 cup chopped bittersweet chocolate
Approximately 20 lady fingers or champagne cookies
2 tsp of cocoa powder or shaved chocolate
5 oz plastic salad tub or 8" cake pan lined with plastic wrap

Combine the first four ingredients in a large bowl and mix by hand with a whisk until stiff. Sprinkle half of the chopped chocolate in the plastic wrap lined container. Spread with half of the cheese mixture and top with a row of tightly spaced cookies (some trimming may be required). Soak the cookies with half of the rum and espresso. Spread the remaining cheese and chocolate over the cookies. Top with a second row of cookies to be soaked with the remaining rum and espresso. Cover with plastic and lid of salad container (or just wrap tightly with plastic wrap if you're using a cake pan instead). Leave in cooler overnight and until ready to serve. Invert onto plate and remove plastic. Dust with cocoa powder or shaved chocolate.

Chef's Note:

This simple Tira Misu can be made after dinner the first night out for dessert on the second night of a camping trip. Whisking the cream by hand is a fun and unexpected group activity in the great outdoors!

# Scrumptious Chocolate Layer Bars
## by Sandy Bahr
## Phoenix

Yield: 3 dozen bars
Preheat: 375°F

2 cups (12 oz package) semi-sweet chocolate chips
1 package (8 ounces) cream cheese
2/3 cup (5.3-ounce can) evaporated milk
1 cup chopped walnuts
1/2 tsp almond extract
3 cups unsifted all-purpose flour
1 1/2 cups sugar
1 tsp baking powder
1/2 teaspoon salt
1 cup butter or margarine, softened
2 eggs
1/2 tsp almond extract

Combine chocolate chips, cream cheese and evaporated milk in medium saucepan. Cook over low heat, stirring constantly, until chips are melted and mixture is smooth. Remove from heat; stir in walnuts and 1/2 teaspoon almond extract. Blend well. Set aside. Combine remaining ingredients in large mixer bowl; blend well with mixer until mixture resembles coarse crumbs. Press half of mixture into greased 13" x 9" pan; spread with chocolate mixture. Sprinkle rest of crumbs over filling. Bake for 35 to 40 minutes or until golden brown. Cool; cut into bars.

# Cheese Cake:
# Easy to Make, Best on the Tongue
## by Dorothy McCarthy
## Phoenix

Preheat: 300°F

crust:
10 graham crackers, crushed
3 oz melted butter

filling:
16 oz cream cheese, room temperature
1/2 cup sugar
1 tsp vanilla

frosting:
16 oz sour cream
3 tbsp sugar
1/2 tsp vanilla

You will need a 6.5" diameter spring form pan. If you'd like to make a larger cheesecake, use a 9" diameter spring form pan and double the recipe.

To make the graham cracker crust, mix the crushed graham crackers with the melted butter. Line the bottom and side of your pan with the graham cracker crust mixture. Set aside.

Mix the cream cheese, sugar, and vanilla until smooth. Pour into pan; bake 20 to 25 minutes at 300°F. Remove from oven, then raise oven temperature to 450°F. Let the cheesecake partially cool in the pan and then prepare the frosting.

To make the frosting, mix sour cream, sugar and vanilla. Pour over the partially-cooled cheesecake; bake an additional 5 to 10 minutes at 450°F.

Before serving, cool the cheesecake thoroughly.

# Applesauce Cake
## by Lorene Simons McCarthy
## Phoenix

Preheat: 325°F

1 1/2 cups raisins
Brandy to cover raisins
1 1/2 cups applesauce, unsweetened
1/2 cup butter
1 1/2 cups sugar
1 tsp ground cloves
1 tsp salt
1 tsp ground allspice
1 tsp ground nutmeg
1 tsp cinnamon
2 tsp baking soda
2 1/2 cups flour
1 1/2 cups chopped pecans

Soak raisins in brandy overnight.  Heat the applesauce in a heavy saucepan.  Melt butter in the hot applesauce.  Add sugar.  Transfer to a large, heavy bowl.  Sift dry ingredients into applesauce mixture, beating well all the while.  Add nuts and raisins last.  Pour into lightly oiled bread loaf pan and bake for 90 minutes.

# Especially For You Cookies
## by Kathy Lopez
### Prescott

Preheat:  350°F


2 cups of flour (or a combination of grains)
1 tsp salt (salt substitute, sea salt, kosher)
1 tsp baking soda (use baking soda)
1 1/2 cups lubricant (butter, margarine, shortening, vegetable oil)
1 1/2 - 3 cups of sweetener (sugar: brown, raw, or cane; Equal;
         honey; juice; prune puree)
2 eggs (eggs, egg substitute, powdered eggs)
1/2 cup water (sink, tub, garden hose, Evian, juice)
2 tsp flavoring  (vanilla, almond, walnut)
6 cups oatmeal (old fashioned, quick, steel rolled, wheat)
a smattering of nuts (unshelled is preferred), dried fruit, sunflower
         seeds, crushed candies, or chocolate of any kind


Mix ingredients you're using in order listed here.  Drop by teaspoon,
tablespoon or soup ladle onto lightly greased cookie sheets.  Bake
at 350°F for 12 minutes, or until they are as soft or hard as you like
them.

# Pie Crust
## by Kathy McCarthy
## Flagstaff

1/2 cup +1/2 tsp solid vegetable shortening
1 3/4 cups flour
1/4 tsp salt
5 tbsp milk (chilled or room temperature is fine)

As written, this recipe makes enough dough for one lower and one upper crust.

Mix shortening, flour, and salt; do not overwork. Then add milk, only 2 tablespoons at a time. Once milk is incorporated, roll out, place the lower crust into pie plate, and fill with your favorite fruit or custard and top with the remaining crust.

Chef's Note:

This recipe is included with the compliments of my mother, Marian.  It's easy to double this recipe at holiday time, or any time more serious baking is called for.

# Carrot Cake
## by Jim McCarthy
### Flagstaff

Preheat: 350°F

1 cup sugar
3 eggs
1 1/2 Cups vegetable oil
2 tsp vanilla
1 tsp salt
2 cups grated carrots
1 cup chopped apple
1 cup white flour
1 cup whole wheat flour
1 tsp baking soda
1 tsp baking powder
2 tsp cinnamon
1 cup chopped pecans
1 cup golden raisins

Mix sugar, eggs, oil, and vanilla together first. Mix other ingredients in. Put batter into two greased and floured 9" square pans. Bake 35 to 45 minutes. Great without frosting, or see pecan cream cheese frosting recipe below.


Pecan Cream Cheese Frosting

6 oz Cream cheese, room temperature
1 tsp milk
2 tsp vanilla
dash salt
16 oz powdered sugar
1/2 cup chopped pecans

Mix the first four ingredients. Add sugar and mix well. Fold in the pecans. Spread on cake.

# No-Bake Frosty Lemonade Pie
## by Mary Miller
## Tempe

Crust:
1 1/4 cups finely crushed pretzels
1/4 cup sugar
1/2 cup butter or margarine, melted

Filling:
1 quart vanilla ice cream or frozen yogurt, softened
6 oz can frozen lemonade concentrate, thawed
few drops yellow food coloring (optional)

Lightly grease 8" or 9" pie pan. In small bowl, combine pretzel crumbs, sugar, and butter. Press in bottoms and up sides of prepared pie dish. Refrigerate 15 minutes.

In large bowl, combine ice cream/yogurt, lemonade concentrate (and if used, food coloring). Spoon into prepared crust after blending well.

Freeze until firm. Let stand at room temperature a few minutes before cutting and serving.

May be served with sliced strawberries or other favorite fruits, or for those with a chocolate tooth, hot fudge sauce.

# Lemon Rosemary Shortbreads
### Page DeMello
### The Garden Territory
### at The Farm at South Mountain
### Phoenix

Preheat: 325°F

2 cups unbleached, all-purpose flour
3/4 tsp Kosher salt
1/2 lb unsalted butter
1/2 cup granulated sugar (or confectioner's sugar, for finer texture)
3-4 tbsp lemon zest
1 tbsp lemon juice
2 tbsp minced fresh rosemary needles

Sift together flour and Kosher salt; set aside. Cream the butter in mixer for about 3 minutes. Gradually add the sugar, and beat another minute or two. Mix in thoroughly the lemon zest, lemon juice, androsemary. Now add the flour mixture, gradually. That's the dough.

Do not over-beat once the flour is in; instead, dump the dough onto a piece of wax paper and knead and fold it just enough to incorporate the flour for a smooth, uniform dough.

Form dough into approximately 1" balls.  Bake for about 20 minutes; they should be just barely brown around the edges (I used insulated cookie sheets).  Optional garnish:  While still warm but not hot, poke a small hole with a toothpick at the center of each cookie and insert a tiny sprig of fresh rosemary.  You could also process some sugar with more lemon zest until almost powdery, and roll the warm cookies in that.

Chilling the formed cookies before baking will help them hold their round shape.  The dough can also be baked in a round or square pan, or a shortbread mold, and cut into squares or wedges.  If chilled, it can be rolled and cut out into leaf shapes.

# German Buttercream Torte
## by Renate Sweat
## Phoenix

Preheat: 375°F

4 eggs (room temperature)
2 tbsp water
3/4 cup sugar
1/2 tsp vanilla
1 cup flour
2/3 cup cornstarch
1 tbsp baking powder
1/2 cup jam (red and tart)
1 lb butter
1 large package vanilla pudding
1/2 cup sugar
2 tbsp cornstarch
2 cups milk

Line the bottoms of two 8" or 9" round cake pans with wax paper. Separate eggs carefully, beat whites until very firm, add 1/4 cup of the sugar to the egg snow. In second bowl beat the egg yolks, water, and other 1/2 cup sugar and vanilla till very fluffy. Carefully put the egg snow on top of the yolk mixture and sift flour, cornstarch and baking powder on top. Stir together by hand to form smooth dough. Bake immediately for 30 minutes. Wait 10 minutes, then turn cakes out to cool on a rack. Cut each cake into 2 or 3 layers.

For the frosting/filling, cook pudding as directed, adding the cornstarch and sugar to the pudding powder. Cool completely, stirring to keep skin from forming. Whip butter with electric mixer until very fluffy, add cold pudding a little at a time. Spread onto cake layers (you can add a layer of jam to 2 or 3 layers, if desired). Frost cake all over and decorate the top using a pastry decorating bag and tip. Store covered in refrigerator.

Variation: Add 1/4 cup of cocoa to half of the buttercream filling.

# Tiramisu
## by Renate Sweat
### Phoenix

Yield: about 16 servings

1 cup powdered sugar
16 oz reduced fat cream cheese
12 oz frozen whipped topping, thawed
2/3 cup sugar
1/3 cup water
4 egg whites
3/4 cup hot water
An additional 1 tbsp sugar
2 tbsp finely ground coffee
2 tbsp coffee liqueur
20 ladyfingers, graham crackers, or tea biscuits
2 tbsp unsweetened cocoa

Soften cream cheese and mix with powdered sugar with electric handmixer. Add 2/3 of the whipped topping with a spatula and fold in. Combine 2/3 cup sugar, 1/3 cup water and 4 egg whites and pour into the top chamber of a double boiler over simmering water. Beat at a high speed with mixer until stiff peaks form. Remove from heat and gently fold into cream cheese mixture. In a separate bowl, combine hot water with sugar and coffee, then cool and add liqueur.

Arrange half of the cookies on bottom of 9" x 13" dish (or similar sized pan). Pour half of coffee mixture over them. Spread 1/2 of cheese mixture on cookies and repeat procedure. Gently spread the rest of the whipped topping over the top layer and dust with cocoa. Cover with plastic wrap and chill at least 2 hours, and/or freeze for 2 hours, so it will cut cleanly (and travel easily in hot weather).

Recipe can easily be cut in half for a smaller 8" x 8" dish, but if you prepare as written, leftovers freeze well for up to two weeks.

# Chocolate Chips Brownies
Mary Miller
Tempe

Yield: 16 brownies
Preheat: 350°F

1 19.8 oz package fudge brownies
1/2 cup vegetable oil
2 large eggs
1/4 cup coffee liqueur
1 1/2 cups semisweet chocolate chips (about 9 oz.)
1 cup chopped pecans

Lightly butter 9" x 9" x 2" metal baking pan. Place brownie mix in bowl. Add oil, eggs, and liqueur, whisking until blended.

Stir in chips and nuts. Transfer batter to prepared pan. Bake until slightly puffed and tester inserted into center comes out with some moist crumbs attached, about 35 minutes. Cool, cut and serve.

# P-Nutty Apple Pie
## by Bertha Cook
## Cornville

Preheat: 400°F

One pastry-lined pie pan
6 apples
2 tbsp lemon juice
1 cup sugar
1/3 tsp cinnamon
1/2 cup crunchy peanut butter
1 cup sour cream
1/4 cup crushed peanuts

Peel and slice apples into a large bowl, then sprinkle with lemon juice. Set aside.

Mix sugar, flour, cinnamon and peanut butter. Add to apples and stir to coat. Turn into a pastry-lined pan. Spread top of apple mixture with sour cream and sprinkle with crushed peanuts. Bake for 25 minutes, then lower temperature to 350°F and keep baking until apples are tender, about 25 minutes more.

# Lemon Supreme Cake
## by Bertha Cook
### Cornville

Preheat:  350°F

1 box lemon cake mix
3 oz package lemon gelatin
4 eggs
3/4 cup water
3/4 cup salad oil
1 lb. powdered sugar
Juice of 3 lemons
1 tsp grated lemon zest

Combine cake mix, gelatin, eggs, and water.  Beat 3 minutes. Add oil, beat 3 minutes more.  Pour into lightly greased and floured 12" x 9" x 2" pan and bake for 35 minutes.

Mix powdered sugar, lemon juice and grated zest together.  As soon as cake is out of the oven, prick entire surface with fork and spread at once with glaze.  Serve when cooled.

Alternate glaze:
3/4 lb powdered sugar
Juice of 3 limes

Follow instructions as above.

# Kevon's Cheesecake
## by Krishna Ruddick
## Detroit, Michigan (formerly of Tempe)

Preheat: 350°F

Crust:
1 1/2 cups graham crackers, crushed
1/2 cup softened butter
2 tbsp sugar

Filling:
24 oz cream cheese
1 1/2 cups sugar
5 eggs
2 tbsp vanilla

Mix ingredients for crust by hand and press into the bottom of a spring form cheesecake pan. Set aside.

Mix filling ingredients in order with a low setting on your hand mixer – just until all ingredients are incorporated. Pour into the pan.

Bake for approximately 1 hour. The top of the cheesecake will be springy.

*"If more of us valued food and cheer and song above hoarded gold, it would be a merrier world."*

J. R. R. Tolkien

# Cooking Measurements and Equivalents

# Imperial-to-Metric Equivalents

| Weight | | Volume | |
|---|---|---|---|
| Imperial | Metric | Imperial | Metric |
| 1/2 oz | 15 g | 1/4 tsp | 1.25 ml |
| 1 oz | 25 g | 1/2 tsp | 2.5 ml |
| 1 3/4 oz | 50 g | 1 tsp | 5 ml |
| 2 3/4 oz | 75 g | 2 tsp | 10 ml |
| 3 1/2 oz | 100 g | 1 tbsp/3 tsp | 15 ml |
| 4 1/2 oz | 125 g | 2 tbsp/1 fl oz | 30 ml |
| 5 1/2 oz | 150 g | 3 tbsp | 45 ml |
| 6 oz | 175 g | 2 fl oz/ 1/4 cup | 50 ml |
| 7 oz | 200 g | 3 1/2 fl oz | 100 ml |
| 8 oz | 225 g | 4 fl oz/ 1/2 cup | 125 ml |
| 10 1/2 oz | 300 g | 7 fl oz | 200 ml |
| 11 1/2 oz | 325 g | 8 fl oz/ 1 cup | 225 ml |
| 12 oz | 350 g | 9 fl oz | 250 ml |
| 14 oz | 400 g | 10 fl oz | 300 ml |
| 15 oz | 425 g | 14 fl oz | 400 ml |
| 1 lb | 450 g | 16 fl oz/ 2 cups | 450 ml |
| 1 lb 2 oz | 500 g | 18 fl oz | 500 ml |
| 1 lb 10 oz | 750 g | 21 fl oz | 600 ml |
| 2 lb 4 oz | 1 kg | 24 fl oz/ 3 cups | 675 ml |
| 2 lb 12 oz | 1.25 kg | 25 fl oz | 700 ml |
| 3 lb 5 oz | 1.5 kg | 4 cups | 900 ml |
| 4 lb 8 oz | 2 kg | 4 1/2 cups | 1 liter |
| 5 lb | 2.25 kg | 6 3/4 cups | 1.5 liters |
| 5 lb 8 oz | 2.5 kg | 9 cups | 2 liters |
| 6 lb | 2.7 kg | 11 cups | 2.5 liters |
| 6 lb 8 oz | 3 kg | 13 cups | 3 liters |

Source: Christine France's *Cooking Hints & Tips* (Dorling Kindersley Ltd., London, 1997).

| Oven Temperature Equivalents* | | | |
|---|---|---|---|
| Common Description | Fahrenheit | Celsius | Typical Uses |
| Cool | 225-250° | 110-120° | Warming |
| Warm | 275-300° | 140-150° | Slow cooking |
| Moderate | 325-350° | 170-180° | Baked goods |
| Fairly Hot | 375-400° | 190-200° | Baked goods Meats/Poultry |
| Hot | 425-450° | 220-230° | Meats/Poultry |
| Very Hot | 475° | 240° | Meats/Poultry |

Source: Christine France's *Cooking Hints & Tips* (Dorling Kindersley Ltd., London, 1997).

A note on convection ovens:

You must reduce cooking times in convection ovens by 5-10 minutes per hour or reduce the temperature called for in the recipe by 20-50°F (10-20°C), since convection ovens cook faster. Your best guides are your oven's instruction handbook and experience.

- - - - - - - - - - - - - - - -

* The formulae needed to convert precise temperatures on your own are:

/ means divide, * means multiply, - means subtract, + means to add and = is equal. Tc = temperature in Celsius, Tf = temperature in Fahrenheit.

Fahrenheit to Celsius: **Tc = (5/9)*(Tf-32)**
For example, to convert 98.6°F into Celsius, first subtract 32 from the Fahrenheit temperature to get 66.6. Then you multiply 66.6 by five-ninths to get 37°C.

Celsius to Fahrenheit: **Tf = ((9/5)*Tc)+32**
For example, to convert 100°C into Fahrenheit, first multiply the Celsius temperature reading by nine-fifths to get 180. Then add 32 to 180 and get 212°F.

Source: USAToday.com

# Web-Based Resources
## for Conservation,
## Slow Food,
## and Points in Between

For an excellent and frequently updated list of the farmers' markets closest to home, go to www.localharvest.org.

For more recipes, clues on the freshest seasonal vegetables and fruit in the Southwest, or to sign up for home delivery of certified organic vegetables grown by small farmers (500 acres or less) in Arizona and California, go to www.boxedgreens.com.

To find out more information about preserving Arizona's native foods, go to www.nativeseeds.org.

To find out more about local conservation issues, go to http://arizona.sierraclub.org.

To find out more about Slow Food USA, which has three Arizona chapters (Flagstaff, Phoenix, and Tucson), go to www.slowfoodusa.org/contact/index.html.

# Books for Your Palate

This book wouldn't have been possible – nor would it be complete – without the somewhat eclectic smattering of food writing that I pass on to you below.

In addition to a heaping serving of what I consider essential to a basic cooking library, the list also offers a pinch of instruction on how to find, grow or prepare foods native to the Sonoran Desert region, a cup of robust love for food, a dash of ethnobotany (the study of how humans use plants), and a measure of hope for improving our society's relationship with food – for the sake of our health, the planet, and our collective psyche.

– R.H.G.

## Cookbooks and Books of Interest on Cooking Basics:

*The Way to Cook*, by Julia Child with photographs by Jim Scherer and Brian Leatheart (Knopf).

*Dictionary of Cuisine (Le Grand Dictionnaire de Cuisine), by Alexandre Dumas* (my edition is the 1958 Avon Books paperback; original publication date is 1873).

*Food Lover's Companion:  Comprehensive Definitions of Over 6,000 Food, Wine and Culinary Terms, 3rd Edition*, by Sharon Tyler Herbst (Barron's).

*American Indian Cooking: Recipes from the Southwest*, by Carolyn Niethammer (University of Nebraska Press).

*Food of the Southwest Indian Nations: Traditional & Contemporary Native American Recipes*, by Lois Ellen Franks (Ten Speed Press).

*The Inquisitive Cook: How a Pinch of Curiosity Can Improve Your Cooking*, by Anne Gardiner and Sue Wilson with the San Francisco Exploratorium (Owl Books).

*Larissa's Bread Book: Baking Bread and Telling Tales with Women of the American South*, by Lorraine Johnson-Coleman and illustrated by Katherine Sandoz.

*Southwest Kitchen Garden*, by Kim Nelson and illustrated by Cynthia Miller (Treasure Chest Books).

*The Tassajara Bread Book*, by Edward Espe Brown (Shambhala Press).

*The Tumbleweed Gourmet:  Cooking with Wild Southwestern Plants*, by Carolyn J. Niethammer and illustrated by Jenean Thomson (University of Arizona Press).

## Thoughts on Contemporary Food Issues:

*Coming Home to Eat:  The Pleasures and Politics of Local Foods*, by Gary Nabhan (Norton Books).

*Fast Food Nation: The Dark Side of the All-American Meal*, by Eric Schlosser (Houghton Mifflin Books).

*Slow Food: Collected Thoughts on Taste, Tradition, and the Honest Pleasures of Food*, edited by Carlo Petrini (Chelsea Green Publishing).

"An Animal's Place," by Michael Pollan (*New York Times Magazine*, November 10, 2002)

**Food and Cooking History:**

*Harvest of the Cold Months: The Social History of Ice and Ices*, by Elizabeth David (Viking Press).

*Ladyfingers and Nun's Tummies: A Lighthearted Look at How Foods Got Their Names*, by Martha Barnette (Vintage Books).

*Perfection Salad: Women and Cooking at the Turn of the Century*, by Laura Shapiro (Modern Library).

*The Physiology of Taste, Or, Meditations on Transcendental Gastronomy*, by Jean Anthelme Brillat-Savarin and translated by M.F.K. Fisher (Counterpoint Books).

*Plant Kingdoms: The Photographs of Charles Jones*, by Sean Sexton and Robert Flynn Johnson (Smithmark Press).

**Food Memoirs of Note:**

*Between Meals,* by A.J. Liebling (Modern Library).

*The Gastronomical Me,* by M.F.K. Fisher (North Point Press).

*Songbirds, Truffles, and Wolves: An American Naturalist in Italy,* by Gary Nabhan (Penguin Books).

*Tender At the Bone: Growing Up At the Table* and *Comfort Me With Apples,* both by Ruth Reichl (Random House).

**Ethnobotanical Works:**

*The Botany of Desire: A Plant's Eye View of the World,* by Michael Pollan (Random House Books).

*Gathering the Desert,* by Gary Nabhan and illustrated by Paul Mirocha (University of Arizona Press).

*Food Plants of the Sonoran Desert,* by Wendy Hodgson (University of Arizona Press).

*Wild Foods of the Sonoran Desert,* by Kevin Dahl (Arizona-Sonora Desert Museum Press).

**Slow Food Resources:**

*The Art of Eating: A Quarterly Journal* by Edward Behr, available on line by going to www.artofeating.com, by calling 800/495-3944, or by writing to Ed Behr directly at Box 242, Peacham, VT  05862.

*Fresh, Organic and Native Foods Produced on the Colorado Plateau: A Directory of Eco-Regional Food Sustainability, 2nd Edition*, co-edited by Lauren Rentenbach and Gary Nabhan (NAU Center for Sustainable Environments).  Nearly one hundred wholesale and retail local food outlets from the Four Corners region are listed.

Request a free copy by going to www.environment.nau.edu/publications/index.htm. You can also mail your request to the Center for Sustainable Environments at Northern Arizona University, Box 5765, Flagstaff, AZ 86011-5765.